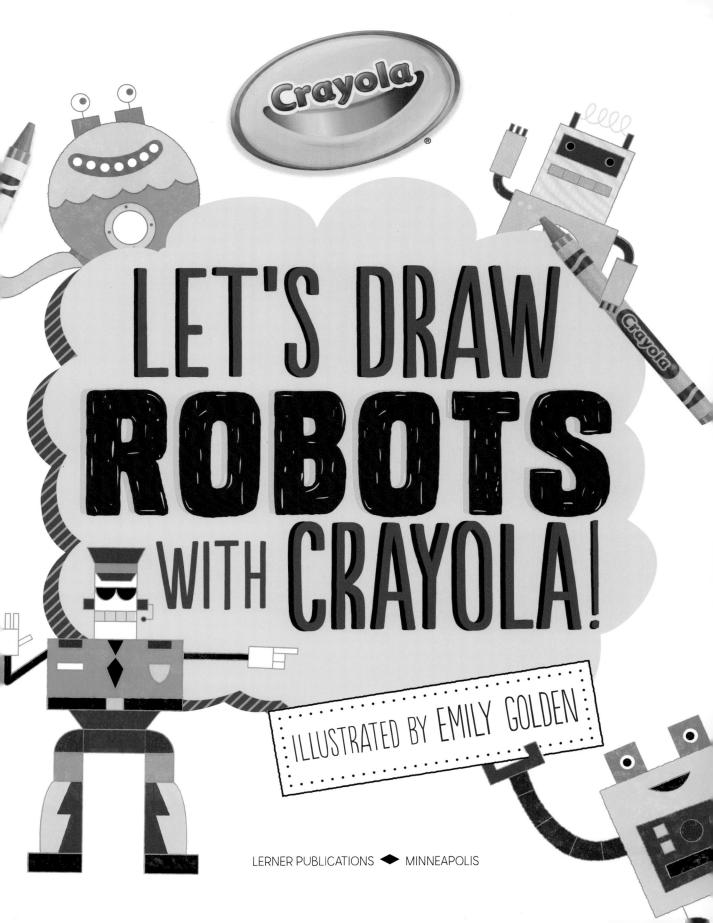

LET'S DRAW ROBOTS WITH CRAYOLA!

ILLUSTRATED BY EMILY GOLDEN

LERNER PUBLICATIONS ◆ MINNEAPOLIS

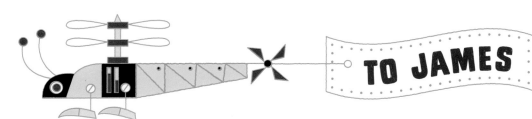

TO JAMES

© 2018 Crayola, Easton, PA 18044-0431. Crayola Oval Logo, Crayola, Serpentine Design, Radical Red, Carnation Pink, Laser Lemon, Inchworm, Screamin' Green, Wild Blue Yonder, Denim, and Purple Heart are registered trademarks of Crayola used under license.

Official Licensed Product
Lerner Publications Company
A division of Lerner Publishing Group, Inc.
241 First Avenue North
Minneapolis, MN 55401 USA

For reading levels and more information, look up this title at www.lernerbooks.com.

Main body text set in Billy Infant Regular 24/30.
Typeface provided by SparkyType.

Library of Congress Cataloging-in-Publication Data

Names: Golden, Emily (Illustrator), illustrator. | Crayola (Firm)
Title: Let's Draw Robots with Crayola®! / illustrated by Emily Golden.
Description: Minneapolis : Lerner Publications, 2018. | Series: Let's draw with crayola®! | Includes bibliographical references. | Audience: Ages 4-9. | Audience: K to Grade 3.
Identifiers: LCCN 2017004833 (print) | LCCN 2017016081 (ebook) | ISBN 9781512497786 (eb pdf) | ISBN 9781512432961 (lb : alk. paper)
Subjects: LCSH: Robots in art—Juvenile literature. Drawing—Technique—Juvenile literature.
Classification: LCC NC825.R56 (ebook) | LCC NC825.R56 D73 2018 (print) | DDC 704.9/49629892—dc23

LC record available at https://lccn.loc.gov/2017004833

Manufactured in the United States of America
1-41827-23787-5/16/2017

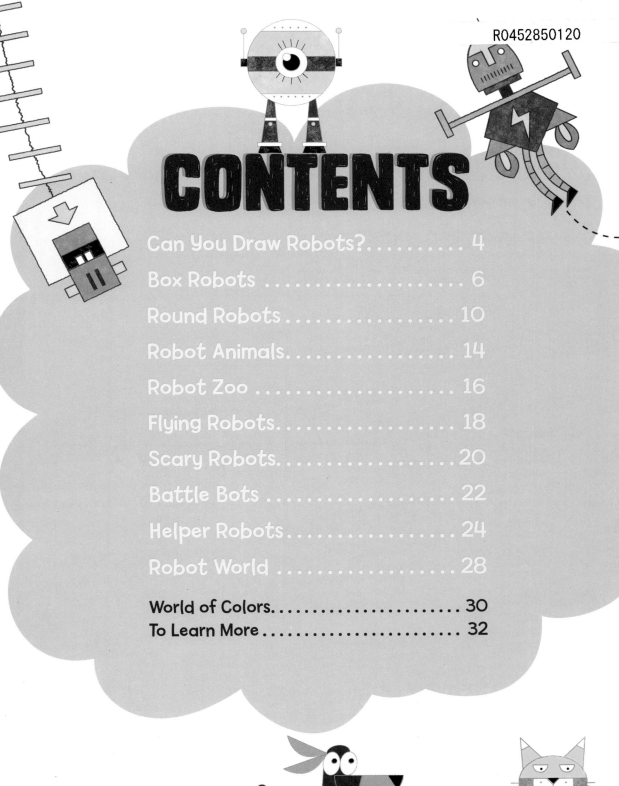

CONTENTS

CAN YOU DRAW ROBOTS?

You can if you can draw shapes! Use the shapes in the box at the top of each page to draw the robot parts. Put the parts together in your drawing to make a battle bot or a robotic firefighter. Or use the parts to make your own robot!

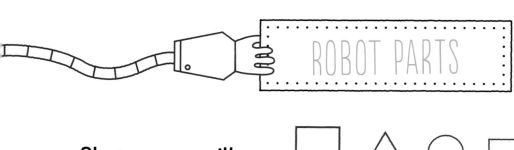

Shapes you will use:

square   triangle   circle   rectangle   half circle

Eyes

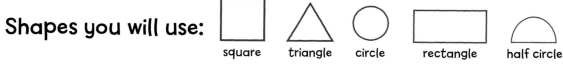

  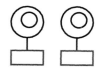 

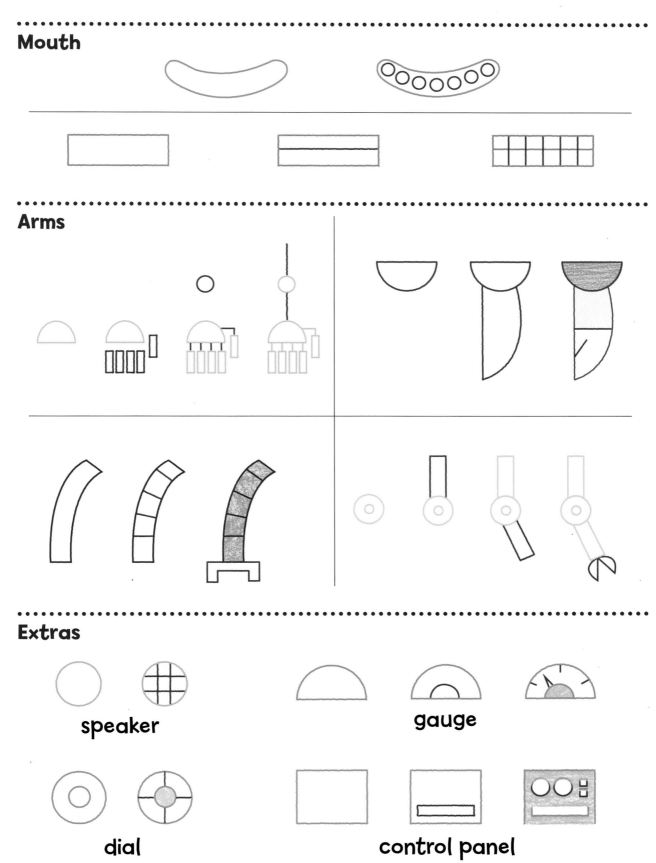

Mouth

Arms

Extras

speaker

gauge

dial

control panel

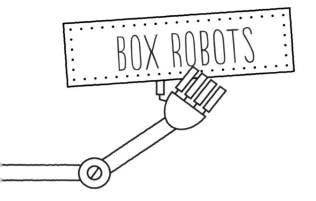

Uni-Wheelie

  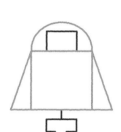 

Cubey

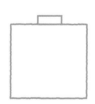 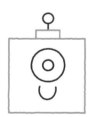 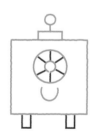  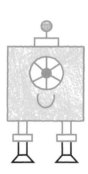

Radar

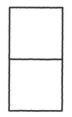 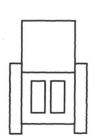 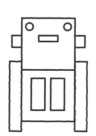 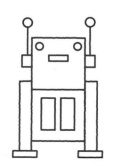 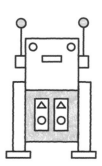

Crabot

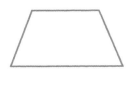

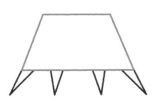

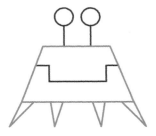

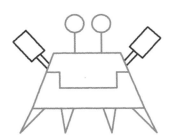

Stomper

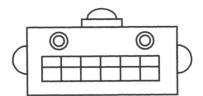

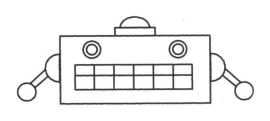

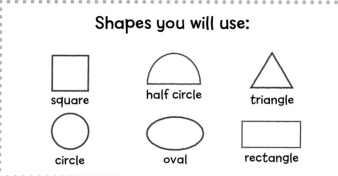

Shapes you will use:

square · half circle · triangle · circle · oval · rectangle

Gearz

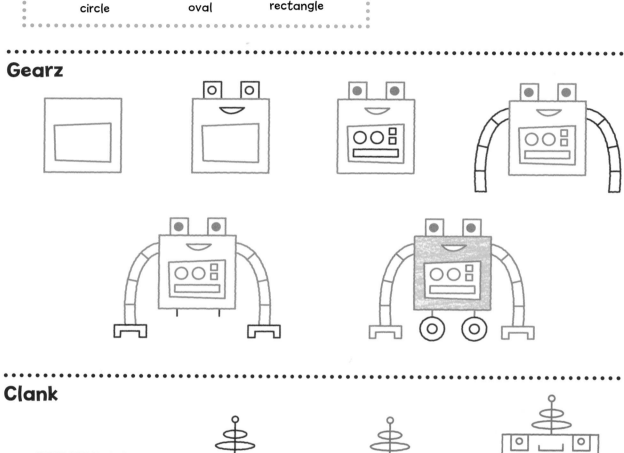

Clank

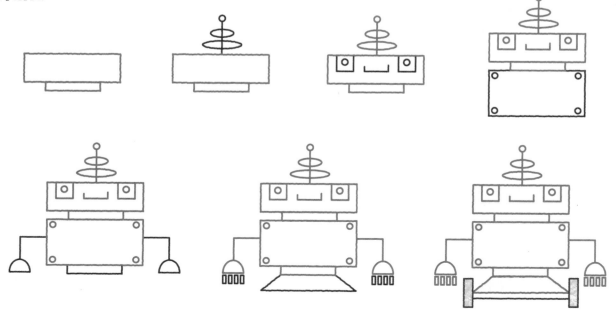

8

Cosmo

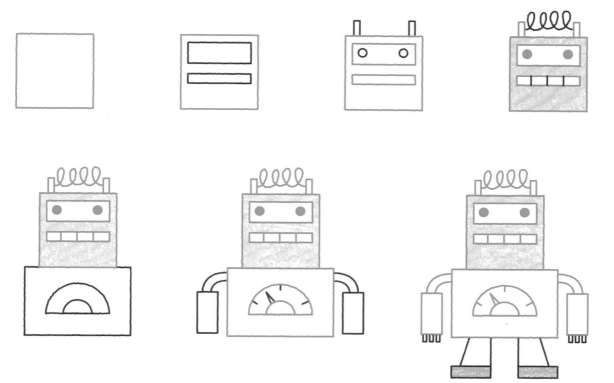

Popper

9

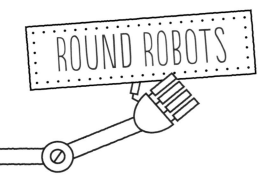

ROUND ROBOTS

Wheelie

Roller

 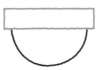 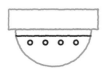 

 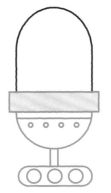 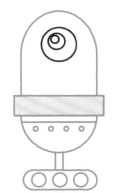 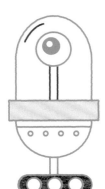

Tum-Tum

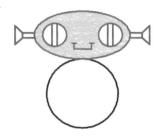 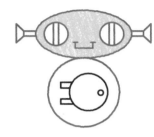 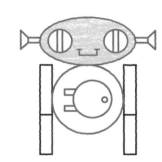 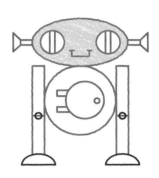

Mr. Minute

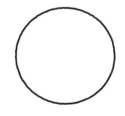 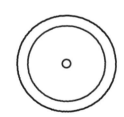  

11

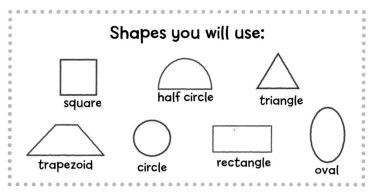
EyeSpy

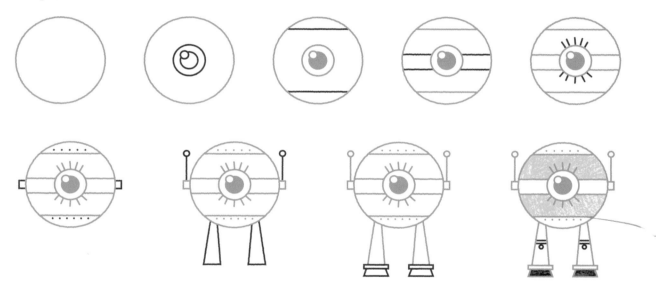

Dot

Turbo Tom

Tentacool

 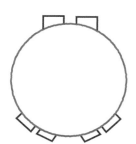  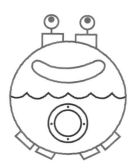

 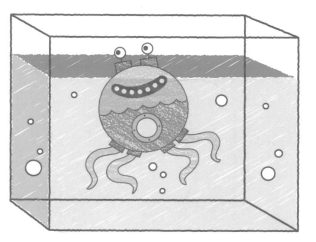

13

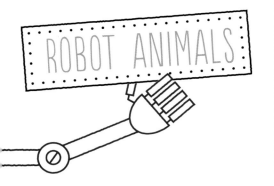

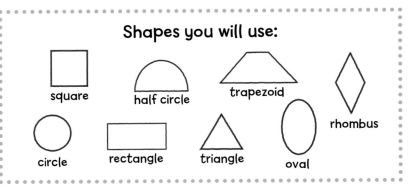

Shapes you will use:

square
half circle
trapezoid
rhombus
circle
rectangle
triangle
oval

Rad Rabbit

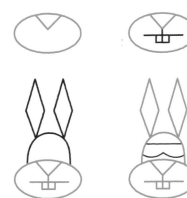

Rufus

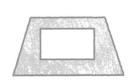

WOOF!

Fischer

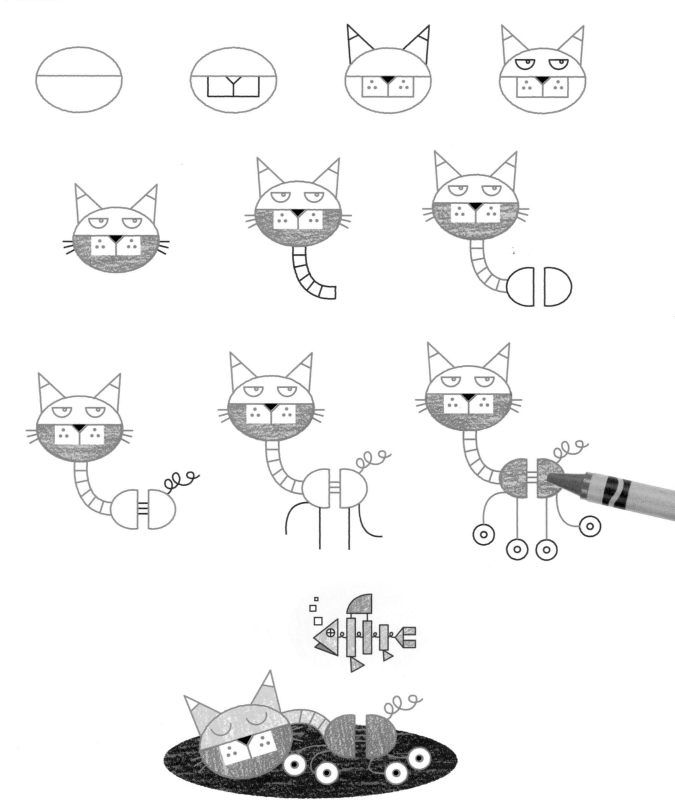

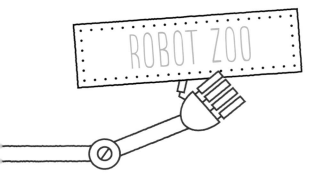

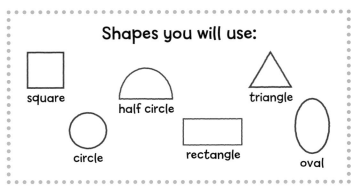

Shapes you will use:

square

half circle

triangle

circle

rectangle

oval

Robo Panda

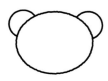   

Mr. Mane

16

Shorty

 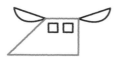 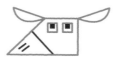 

 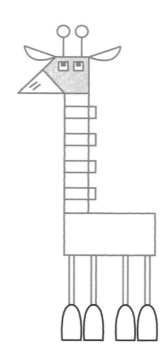 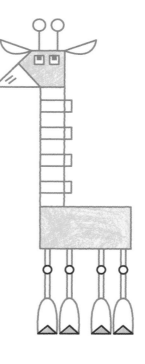

17

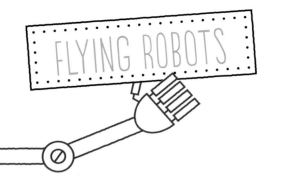

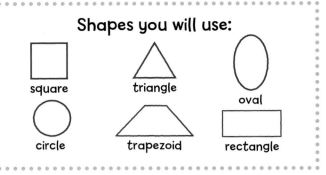

Shapes you will use:

square · triangle · oval · circle · trapezoid · rectangle

Grabber

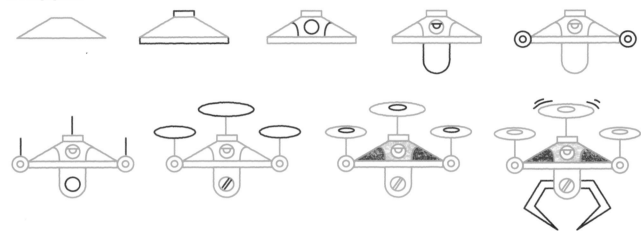

Rocket Man

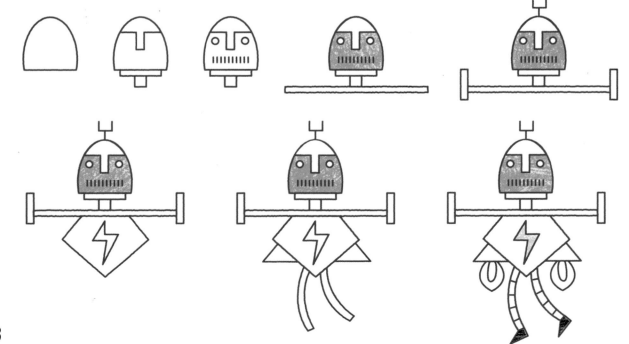

18

Bug

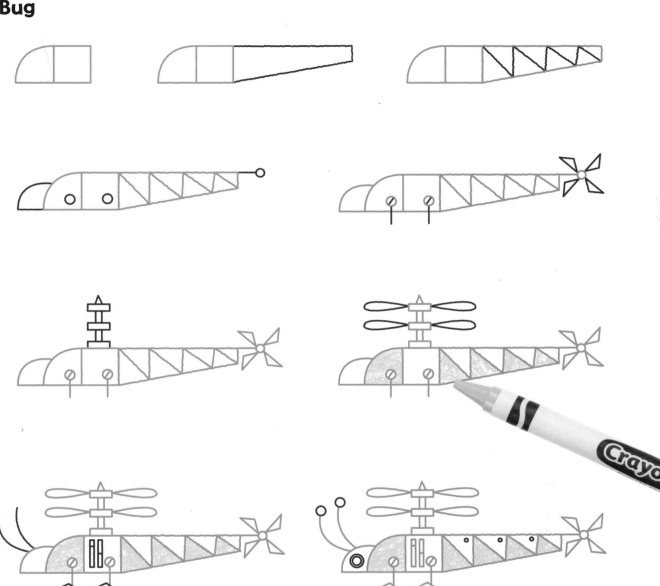

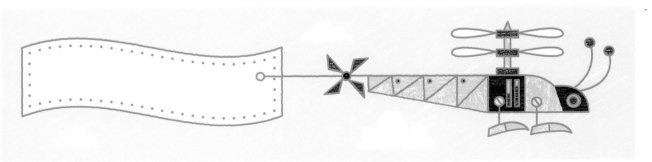

19

SCARY ROBOTS

Shapes you will use:

square   circle   half circle   triangle

rectangle   trapezoid   oval

Spideroid

Vampixel

20

Frankenbot

 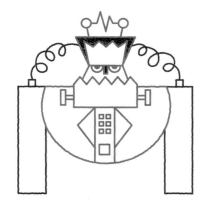 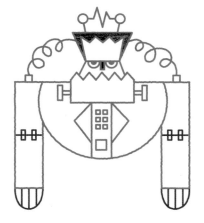

  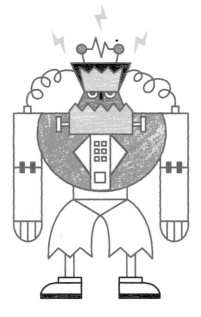

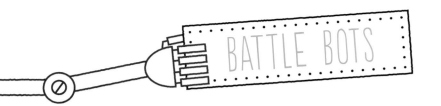

Juggernaut

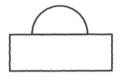

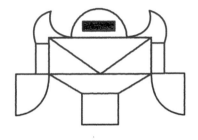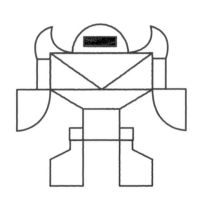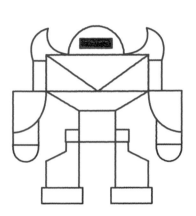

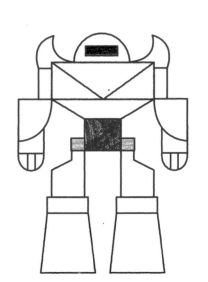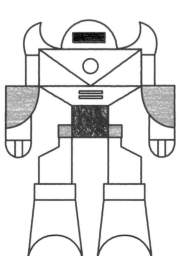

Sir Terrobyte

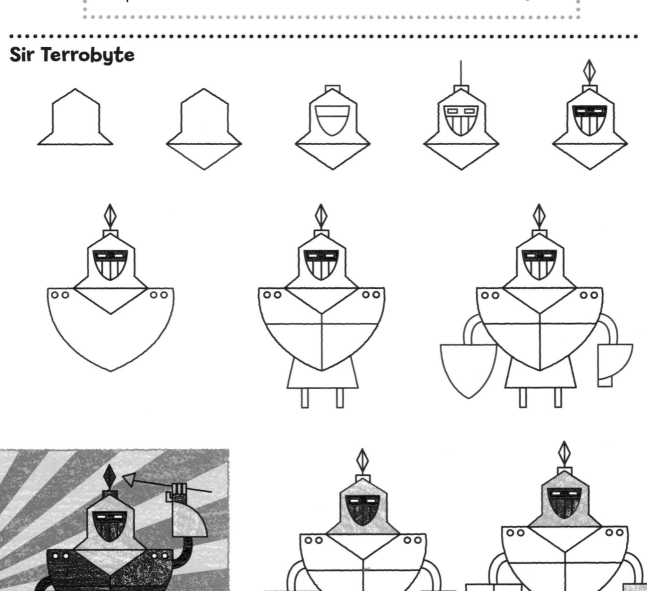

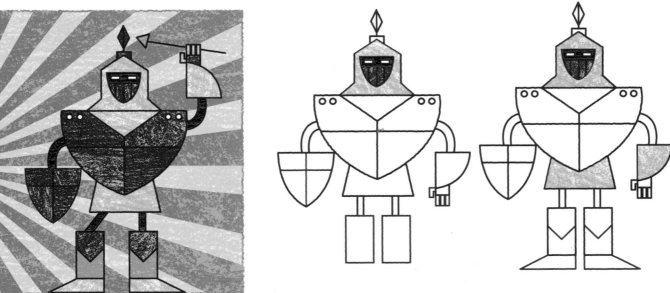

23

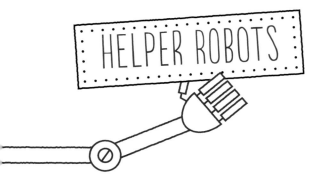

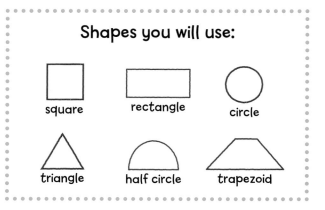

Shapes you will use:

square rectangle circle

triangle half circle trapezoid

Copper 911

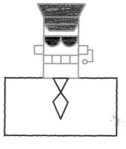 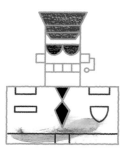 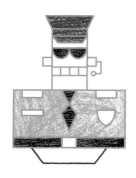 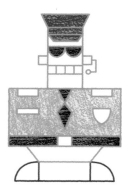

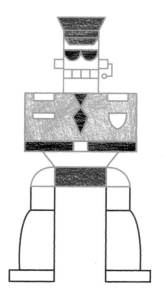 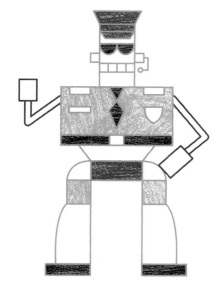 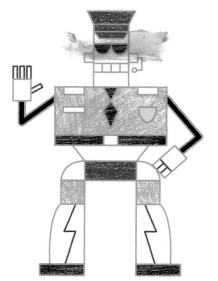

24

Eraze-a-Blaze

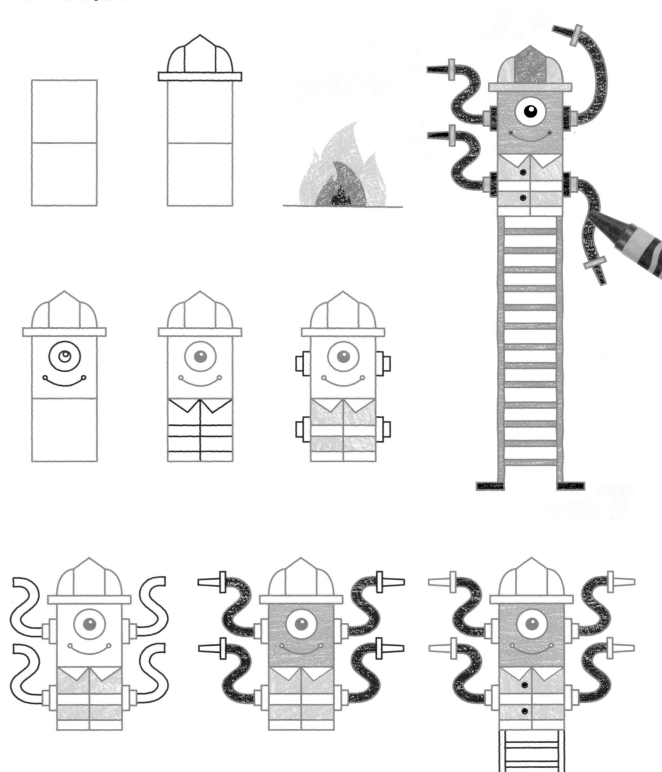

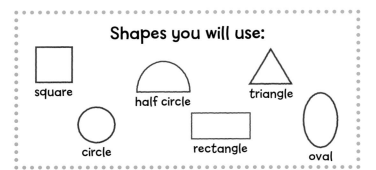

square
half circle
triangle
circle
rectangle
oval

Digger

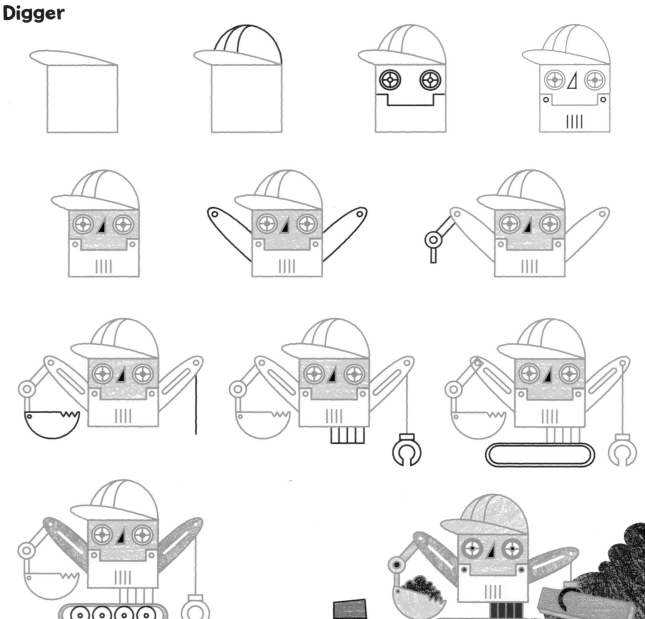

Chefie

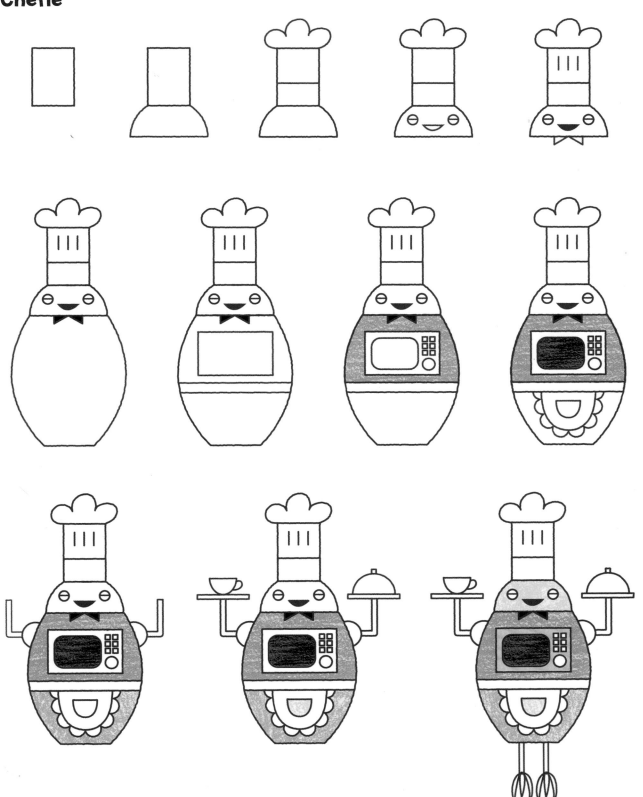

27

WORLD OF COLORS

The world is full of colors! Here are some of the Crayola® crayon colors used in this book. What colors will you use to draw your next robot?

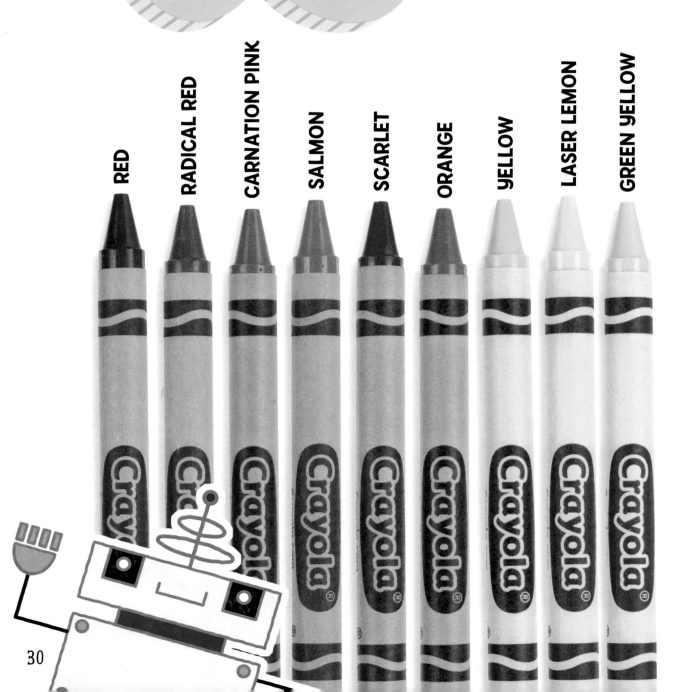

RED

RADICAL RED

CARNATION PINK

SALMON

SCARLET

ORANGE

YELLOW

LASER LEMON

GREEN YELLOW

TIME FOR DRAWING!

INCHWORM

SCREAMIN' GREEN

ROBIN'S EGG BLUE

SKY BLUE

WILD BLUE YONDER

PERIWINKLE

CORNFLOWER

DENIM

PURPLE HEART

PLUM

TO LEARN MORE

Books

Bergin, Mark. *It's Fun to Draw Robots and Aliens*. New York: Sky Pony, 2014.
Follow the step-by-step instructions in this book to learn how to draw more robots and aliens too.

Masiello, Ralph. *Ralph Masiello's Robot Drawing Book*. Watertown, MA: Charlesbridge, 2011.
Get more practice using shapes to design your robots with this drawing book.

Torres, Jickie. *Robots*. Irvine, CA: Walter Foster, 2015.
Watch a drawing come alive in this fun story about a robot named Bop!

Websites

Single-Shape Drawing
http://www.crayola.com/crafts/singleshape-drawing-craft/
Visit this website to try drawing a robot using just one type of shape.

Tracing Shapes
http://www.guruparents.com/support-files/tracing-shapes-worksheet.pdf
Use this page to get more practice drawing shapes. Start by tracing the shapes on the page, and then move on to drawing them yourself!